AF335527

The Seasons
of a Short, Holy Life

MEMORABLE MUSINGS
OF A POET PRIEST

REV. DUNCAN REILLY, O. CARM.
EDITED BY KENNETH E. NOWELL

Vero House
Publishing

The Seasons of a Short, Holy Life
Memorable Musings of a Poet Priest
by Rev. Duncan Reilly
Edited by Kenneth E. Nowell

Copyright © 2013 Jeanne Reilly

Vero House Publishing, Corp.
5460 Corsica Place
Vero Beach, FL 32967
www.VeroHousePublishing.com
Telephone or fax: **888-292-7160**
Email: admin@VeroHousePublishing.com.

**Published: July 16, 2013,
the feast of
Our Lady of Mount Carmel**

Printed in the United States of America.

ISBN: 978-0-9886539-5-5

Table of Contents

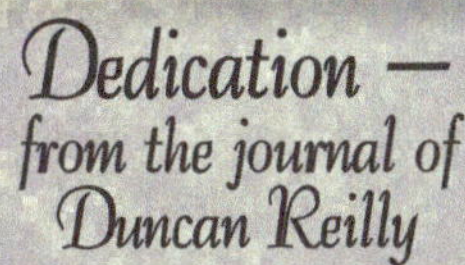

Dedication —
from the journal of
Duncan Reilly

God has given me soul and body, through Mother and Father, who nourished me and brought me up to be what I am. God made me out of His love, they raised me out of theirs.

Walter Henry Reilly

Matilda Malcolm Reilly

Editor's Foreword

He had a quick wit, sharp mind and the kind of endearing personality that attracted nicknames, not usually associated with a man of the cloth. Some called him Dunc, but family kept the habit of using Goog and Googie. Fellow seminarians knew him as the pool hustler and, later, his students fondly labeled him "hot-rod." His religious titles ranged from frater to brother to father. But Duncan Reilly also deserved the title of poet, because he never lost his love of submitting his clever or touching observations to the discipline of the rhyme.

Most of young Duncan's written works were humorous and filled with unbridled ambition for serving Christ. They were usually dated, and he posted "Maria!" above each poem. He must have found inspiration during the late night quiet because he often noted that a creative work had been completed in the wee hours of the morning.

Naturally, the emotional and Spiritual seasons of his short, holy life were often expressed through those written words. But Duncan's faith never waivered, from the light-hearted springtime of adolescence – humorously skewering boring teachers or dreaming about possible girl friends – to his winter years, dominated by endless treatments for Hodgkins Disease. In fact, with 10 months still to live, he playfully mocked his dire situation in a letter that cataloged his trials: "...Cobalt 60 radiation on the lungs and hip ... about 170 x-ray treatments on 16 different areas ... 40 doses of nitrogen mustard, 1 of thiotepa ... a case of shingles requiring hospitalization, and all the IVPs, GIs, IVs, pneumoperitonneums, bone marrow punctures, and – worst of all – finger sticks for six years. These are my credentials to write a few pious platitudes."

Still, with the love, humility and dedication of a victim soul, he offered to accept sharing in Christ's sacrificial suffering:

Dear God, I accept all things from Your hands – persecution, sickness, insanity , all manner of trial, and death. Only help me to arrive at the fullness of love for You that my heart is capable of. Help me to help myself, and help me to help others. Finally, help me to stop the blurting of my big mouth.

Perhaps Duncan's happiest years were the two that spanned from his ordination, in 1955, to the discovery of his disease. Then, he was blessed to teach the many children that he loved and wrote about so much. However, his short-lived vocation soon left him even unable to administer the Sacraments and that may have haunted him most. In his last year of life, he bemoaned how few Sacraments he had administered, writing, "I had a heck of a time beating down the feeling that I was somehow a flop as a religious and as a priest."

Upon the death of Father Duncan Reilly, his remaining family mourned his passing just as they previously had mourned the untimely deaths of both parents. But, still, from his memorable writings, the family would continue to celebrate the love, wit and wisdom that Googie had brought to the world in his 33 full years of life. For half a century his sisters remained dedicated to organizing boxes full of Duncan's writings, memories and condolence letters into a book of poetry. Now, their undying goal has been accomplished.

Father Duncan Reilly: a priest in this life for less than a decade, but a priest in heaven forever.

Kenneth E. Nowell

SPRING

In the springtime of life, young Duncan Reilly had one burning ambition: to share eternity with God. His family had recognized him as their "little saint" from his earliest years. So, it was not surprising that at just 13 years of age, Duncan left home to pursue his studies at a Carmelite seminary.

He adapted well to the new residence, maintaining his colorful humor, boyish charm and Spiritual ambitions. There, he learned to express his witty observations in poetic verse, a talent he would hone the rest of his life.

In his journal entries and poetry, young Duncan alternated from serious reflections on proper conduct and saintly living, to amusing anecdotes

on life, as seen through the eyes of a precocious boy, impatiently maturing into manhood and sainthood.

Doctor Soporificus*

A pox on all bad teachers,
However bright they be,
For they are bushelled candles
If their students cannot see.

So stuff this in the archive
And let it rest a while.
Posterity will find it.
Perhaps someone will smile.

May he escape the sentiments
That rot the rhymer's pen.
Beware the subject's vices
If he molds the minds of men.

Doctor Soporificus,
A man so scholarly,
That he's exempt from teaching —
Or so it seems to be.

Safe within a sheaf of notes,
A bee within a bloom,
Our Doctor Soporificus
Exudes dogmatic gloom.

He has no continuity,
But buzzes where he will,
And rooting with a nasal snout,
He renders dogma swill.

His flat and slow delivery
Won't help the students think
And so the pupils long for sleep
But try hard not to blink.

His every class, a research quilt,
A patchwork from the authors.
With this, he daily blankets us,
But, for knowledge, he never bothers.

* Soporific means sleep inducing.

Journal entry:
October 9, 1950

Today I took an unnecessary nap at 2:00 PM and didn't get up when I should have. Fr. Malachy woke me at 2:50, informed me that study began at 2:45, and that I should kneel out this afternoon for meditation. It occurs to me that all my irresoluteness – not getting up in the afternoon when I intend to, and not studying first and recreating later – all this is a breach of obedience and, therefore, not to tolerated any longer.

The Angel on
Your Christmas Tree

A tiny pine grew near the spot
Where Jesus Christ was born.
Since it could not go see Our Lord,
It wept and was forlorn.

Then Jesus sent His Angel out
To greet the pine for Him.
The Angel froze atop the tree,
Upon the highest limb.

So sweet he seemed, when Jesus looked,
That Christ was moved to say,
"Little Angel, please remain."
And, there, he sits today.

Journal entry:
April 6, 1952

One of my main troubles is – let us avoid
moral classifications – day-dreaming. As
might be expected, many such dreams fall
into three classes: 1.) me afflicted, 2.) me
afflicted, but victorious, and 3.) "conjec-
tural niceties." They are all wastes of time.

Willie's Confession

I shot an arrow through a hole,
It landed in the puddin' bowl!

Just before our Ma perceived it,
I had hoped to go retrieve it.

But dozing in his fav'rite chair,
Papa might wake and see me there.

So, dodging the risk, off I sped
To hide my guilt in the ol' woodshed.

Laying there, in a wheelbarrow,
I pondered that puddin' and the arrow.

My forlorn heart began athrobbin'.
Then brother Bart came in asobbin':

"Pappy's lies daid on the kitchen floor.
Mammy won't make us puddin' no more!"

I said, "Brother Bart, please tell dear Ma,
It was my arrow that killed poor Pa."

"But serves him right for eatin' it whole.
Now, get me what's left in the puddin' bowl!"

Racing Waiters

The knives and forks were sounding
The meal had just begun.
Two waiters passed the lector stand,
And then began to run.

Their platters were aburnin' hands,
This added to their speed.
Neck and neck, approaching narrows,
Won't someone take the lead?

Too late for asking questions,
Two platters hit the floor.
Too late for vain excuses,
Two waiters wait no more.

Speak, Fairest Season

Spring, fair queen of seasons,
Of all, most gaily dressed,
Who strews the field with flowers
And fills the robin's nest.

Whence comes your life and beauty?
From Autumn's leaves that lay
In death 'neath Winter's snow?
If this is so, then say.

What blood in your veins now courses?
What elixir in them flows?
Sweet Spring, oblige and answer,
Do they pulse with melted snows?

Escalator

You gobble up gum wrappers
And shoestrings without question.
So, I won't worry one little bit
When you whine about indigestion.

Journal entry:
Retreat - June 7, 1950

Walking around after the conference I looked up at the sky and saw the Big Dipper in a position, overheard, as though pouring upon me God's grace. I realized it was Him telling me how much grace I've been receiving and will continue to get (because the Dipper never empties.)

I also realized – for an instant, and imperfectly – God's goodness in choosing me from among all the millions that cover the face of the earth, and in giving me three braces in my three sisters who are always praying for me, another in my dear mother and father, and another in the best and only brother – not best because only.

May God help me to become a better Carmelite through this retreat, and also a saint. Ten days is quite long enough to become a saint if one cooperates constantly with God's grace. But I hope to become a canonized one – that takes longer! But it is God's grace that counts there, too!

The Midnight Oil

I have a test tomorrow,
Story's also due.
Haven't started either yet.
Oh boy, my future's blue.

I had the entire weekend,
But went to shoot some pool.
The time flew by. I know, next time,
I won't be such a fool.

I think I see it clearly, now.
Yes, man was made to toil.
So, on this night, I'll be a man
And burn the midnight oil.

But then I lapsed and fell asleep,
Out by half past ten.
I slept for two short hours.
Then, startled, got up again.

I thought, "Midnight oil you're burning,"
As I trimmed my wicks.
Then I made this promise:
"No rest till half-past six."

I did not break my sincere pledge,
I labored on till dawn.
But couldn't eat my breakfast,
So often did I yawn.

And now, it is all over.
We got our test grades back.
Oh, let me haul away my sorrow
In a potato sack.

My test score was a goose egg.
My story didn't rate.
So as I slumped my shoulders,
I thought, "It must be fate."

But I hadn't rehearsed my Latin
Or studied History.
Why I ever stalled that long
Remains a mystery.

At long last, now, I see the truth
And, from it, I recoil:
You get nowhere in the light of day,
When you've burnt the midnight oil.

Journal entry:
April 30, 1952

One month of school left. (30 days to catch up on studies, and to catch up on self.) In the month to come I will try to be a model Carmelite: prompt, silent, provident, prayerful. Every day is a new experience, a new chance to do better: to meditate better, to attend Mass and receive Him better, to learn more, to become more holy.

Journal entry:
Undated

Nothing is yours but a great debt of Love – and free will. Boast not of the latter, for you have abused it by sinning and adding to your debt of love. Be conscious of your nothingness and you will never be insulted.

Ode to Mt. Carmel

Carmel, O Carmel,
Thy windows need awashing,
Thy halls no longer shine.
Thy scrappy trees and bushes,
For pruning they do pine.

Carmel, O Carmel,
See thou thy untrimmed lawns?
See thou thy sorry plight?
Thy grounds do look quite dingy.
Thy beauty was thy might!

Great Carmel! Mount Carmel,
Return to your past glory.
I've a speech in Greek to face.
Please do us both a favor,
Have a work day in its place!

Cactus, Cactus

Cactus, cactus
On the sill,
All winter long
You've drunk your fill.

You haven't grown
The leastest bit,
'Cause all you do
Is drink and sit.

I often lie
Upon my bed
And wonder if
You're really dead.

Do cacti always
Act like possums,
While they conjure
Pretty blossoms?

So, now that Spring
Is on the way,
Will you now, please,
Just bloom some day?

Amputation

G.P. hemmed.
Patient hawed.
Pills running out.
Surgeon sawed.

Christmas Moon

Cradled 'mid the pine trees
'Neath a sky, dark blue,
Rose the moon one Christmas Eve
Bringing all into view.

Lighting weary travelers
Returning from the towns,
Moon sneered at all the Scrooges
rushing 'round with hurried frowns.

Then a blue-white whisp of smoke
Ascends above the snow,
Rising from a cheerful hearth,
Whose fire now burns quite low.

Moon sees a youngster ask her mom,
As o'er her bed she bows,
"Will I see Santa here, tonight?"
Moon hides behind a cloud.

'Cause that, alone, of all the things
The moon would like to do,
Was, alas, impossible:
Bring Santa into view!

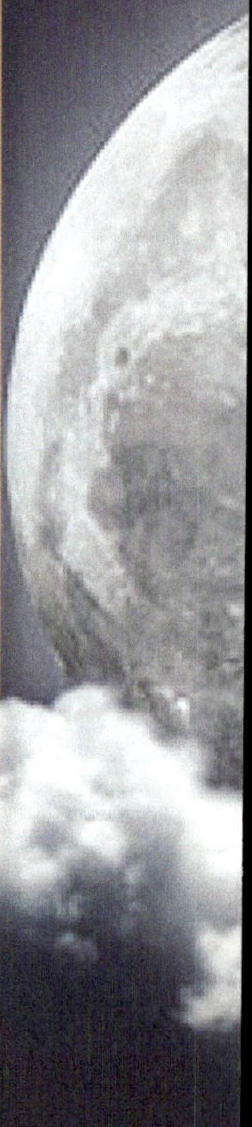

Life in New York City

I spied a ragged beggar,
Back against the wall,
Sprawled upon the pavement,
He voiced a doleful call.

Coins in hand, I hastened by
To fill his empty cup.
I even thought of asking
If he'd come with me and sup.

When I approached, I saw his sign.
The letters had been hazy.
But then I read the honest truth:
"I'm not blind, just lazy."

Journal entry:
Undated

Guard against slovenliness in your cell: dust it every other day with a dust rag and a mop. Don't leave anything out of place, saying, "I'll get that later." The cell will soon be cluttered up and require not a little thoughtfulness, but a load of labor to restore order in it.

Lollipop

Everything's a lollipop,
Times ten times ten times ten.
Yet, treat's diminished every time
Supply exceeds the yen.

So give me all in short supply,
Where none will cloy or satisfy,
Till yen has grown to comprehend
A lollipop without an end.

A Child's Prayer

Midnight Mass had ended,
the Church was rather still.
Wandering up the middle aisle:
a little boy, named Bill.

Spying the crib
Where the Christ Child lay,
He quickened his step
And headed that way.

Then, over the railing
And into the hay,
He knelt by the manger,
As if to pray.

I was nearby
and tip-toed that way
To better hear
What he had to say:

"Jesus, Jesus,
Why lay so still?
I'm right here,
Your best friend, Bill!

"Ask your mother
To come with me.
Please hurry up,
There's a lot to see.

"I have no toys
To give you, Lord,
But we'll have fun
At the ten-cent store.

"We'll watch the train
Rumble 'round the track,
And then see the man
Make it go straight back!"

For a moment, Bill waited,
But no one spoke.
Then silence abdicated,
with a Voice, the quiet broke:

"Believe me, Bill,
I'd love to go.
But mother says
The store is closed."

So, Bill got up
And heaved a sigh,
Genuflected
And waved goodbye.

Time and Eternity

Life is a bowl of cherries
That Time and Eternity eat.
Eternity will settle for the pits,
But Time will consume the meat.

And when the bowl is finally bare
And the cherries are no more,
Time sits back and whistles
While Eternity writes the score.

Just pray your bowl's not empty
The day you pass away.
Leave 'cherries' for your loved ones
From your deeds, in work and play.

Yes, Time shall judge appearance.
But his judgement counts for naught.
Eternity discerns intention,
Whereby our deeds are wrought.

So prune you now your cherry tree
And good habits will bear fruit
Lest someday in Eternity
You'll regret your faults' deep root.

Trickle-Trickle

Born of an icicle
On a mountain peak.
Trick-trickle, trick-trickle,
I soon begin to speak.

Born of an icicle
My friend was melted snow.
Trick-trickle, trick-trickle,
Then I start to flow.

Born of an icicle,
Now much more than a leak.
Trick-trickle, trick-trickle,
Across the plains I streak.

Born of an icicle
I meet new friends galore.
Trick-trickle, trick-trickle,
My voice becomes a roar.

Thru leafless groves I dash
With speed of bird on wing.
Gurgling sun-lit splash,
I cry, "Awake! 'Tis Spring!"

Journal entries:
October, 1950
[After listing his many blessings, particularly regarding his loving and faithful family, Duncan wrote the following:]

God has given me all these and everything else, because He loves me. He loves me because He chooses to, and not because I in any way deserve it. That is why He hasn't stopped giving to me, even though I have given him no return but ungratefulness and sinfulness....

All we have has been given to us and was in no way earned; our vow of Poverty should help us to remember we own nothing, but only have the use of things.

May 7, 1952

Letter from [sister] Jeanne tonight. Mom's tumor was cancer. A year or two will tell whether it spreads. Apparently responding well to treatment.*

*Duncan's mother died on All Souls Day of 1952 as a result of breast cancer, less than six months after this was written.

Mother's Day Memories

Say, Mom, you must remember,
How in days that, now, are gone,
Your youngest son (that's me, Mom)
Was an awful "hanger on."

I wasn't even three, then,
Yet I had a marvelous grip.
I'd often grab your apron strings,
And sometimes make you trip.

But, Mom, you must have known, then,
I didn't mean to hurt you.
I had to show my love, somehow,
To speak was not my virtue.

Happy are those memories, Mom,
Reflecting on family life.
Happier still the lucky man
Who calls you his dear wife.

Now, Pop, I shouldn't mention you.
After all, it's Mother's Day.
But my conscience won't allow it,
Crying, "What would Popper say?"

So Mom and Pop, I'll finish with
My present thoughts unfurled:
You're the best Mom amd Pop,
I have to admit, in the whole wide world!

SUMMER

By the time of Duncan's late-teen years, the parents of his close-knit family had both passed away. His three sisters had become Dominican nuns – two of which were cloistered. Duncan's older brother had started in seminary but eventually chose marriage, instead of the priesthood.

Though Duncan had remained in seminary, his poetry revealed that he was considering future alternatives. Clearly, he had fallen in love – perhaps, more than once – and, occassionally, had felt the pain of rejection. But his Spiritual commitment remained strong and he marvelled at the fact that his cloistered sisters seemed happier each time he saw them.

Judgment

Labeled.
Libeled.
Liable.

I Tutor Her

I tutor her.
She teaches me.
She doesn't charge,
But she's my fee.

Her lessons sting.
They leave an ache.
I'm so enthralled,
They seldom take.

Today's was taught
Without a look.
It hurt so much
I felt the hook.

I'll tutor her,
As she does me.
Ignore the ache
'Cause that's my fee.

Silly Pumpkin

I bought a pumpkin for my love
And brought its smile to life.
Then my love disowned me,
For the orange creation of my knife.

Smile, silly pumpkin. Enjoy her love.
She'll hold you and hug you, perhaps.
Live your short life, under her spell,
Then merrily rot and collapse.

Smile, silly pumpkin, my rival.
Is it each other we slay?
My skillful knife has shortened your life.
I, from envy, decay.

Journal entry:
Ash Wednesday – February 22, 1950.

* Meditate on the Passion.
* Fast well. (Sundays: Feast well.)
* Keep silence at all times: "Let your answers be yea and nay," that is, speak briefly (when spoken to).
* At reception, be sociable.*

*Don't be individual ... be a part of a whole (community). At recreation "mix": the religious state is a communion. Be a good listener. Never broach a subject that will lead to a discussion involving yourself or your accomplishments. Gain from the good examples that are all around you.

Journal entries:
April 30, 1952.

Tomorrow is the first of May. As a Carmelite and as a Catholic, I feel bound to honor Mary in some special way this month for her Glory – which is her Son's – and for my sanctification.

St. Joseph, help me not to let this project die young, like so many other things I have begun and not finished. Holy Spirit, enlighten me, direct me, help me to do the following:

- My meditations will be very definite: one each day on Mary.
- No coffee or tea. (God, help me remember).
- Litany of Humility, daily.
- Rosary at O.L.P. after lunch.
- Rise at 4:45 (or 15 min. early, in honor of B.V.M.) to atone for all the times I've slept late.
- No naps – go to chapel, instead. (Put a chair or something on my bed, as a reminder.)
- Keep the diary.

June 10, 1952.

Last night – long conference on the prayers of ordination; chastity, the vow; a bit about obedience. He says little, talks much. Phooie!

Spirits to Spare

Midnight and moonlight
And Halloween
Find me gazing
At a horrible scene:
Corn shucks and pumpkins,
Witches and cats,
Goblins and gremlins,
Riding on bats.

Each little corn shuck
Foaling black witches,
Every small goblin
Bent over in stitches.
The scarecrow is braving
The frigid breeze,
While cats are eyeing
A moon of green cheese.

Then six little imps
Try stealing a broom.
All six rascals
Are tempting their doom.
My wits affrighted,
I let go a yell,
That sent them all
Scampering to hell.

Scarce had they vanished,
When 'cross the mead
There flashed a horseman
On ebony steed.
Then Father Louis
Quickly disappeared.
He'll not return
For another year.

Angel Michelle

Two years back
God made Michelle
(For a grounded angel,
She walks quite well).

It must have been
A windy night
When her wings blew off
On her maiden flight.

Now, she chatters cherub-talk
all day with God,
A wingless wanderer
On alien sod.

At nap and night time
You might hear her cry,
Complaining to angels
She can no longer fly.

She has learned to like diapers
More than her cloud
For doing the things,
Elsewhere, aren't allowed.

The angels came daily
To laugh and to look
At sweet Michelle's face,
Smeared with breakfast gook.

But one summer night
Her curtains did rustle
When visiting angels
Engaged in a tussle.

They vied to touch
Her Golden hair
To leave just one
Little wing-print there.

Then dawn light did show
From that single curl,
That baby Michelle
Had become a girl.

Now she won't remember —
If she ever knew —
Michelle was an angel
And once, just once, she flew.

Journal entry:
February 4, 1951

There is currently a debate at our table as to whether a man can be reasonably certain that he will be alive tomorrow. If he is not sure, he should live an exemplary life today. But we all know that a day will come when each of us will be reasonably certain of living tomorrow, *but will be wrong!* Still, we refuse to act as perfectly as we might. So it follows that we are either insane or deficient in our knowledge of Christian Doctrine in which we learn that there is Hell and Purgatory.

From an Attic

'Twas afternoon, and like a moon
On a great and tow'ring brink,
The orange-red sun beamed its farewell,
And then began to sink.

And as it set, the sky it wet,
With golden rays of light.
But at my window I still sat
To glimpse a wondrous sight.

At length I caught what I had sought —
The sun's last ray in flight.
Then I got up and lit a lamp,
For all was dark, 'twas night.

Journal entry:
February 4, 1951

Have you ever been self-conscious — felt you were secretly being looked at? laughed at? pitied? cheered? Realize that we are — in the words of St. Paul — a spectacle to men and to angels, and perhaps especially so when at prayer. Angels pity, laugh, jeer, sympathize, cheer and love us — not for our success or failure in prayer, but for our success or failure in *trying to try* to pray.

Die Moldau und Herr Dalmau

Die Moldau iss ein river.
Iss very vide und deep.
Herr Dalmau iss ein author
Vott pudz us all to schleep!

Die Moldau und Herr Dalmau
Dey vander much die zame.
Dey boths juz babble on und on,
Und dots deir claim to fame.

Die von haz got a channel
Vrom die mountains to die zee.
Und venn it goez rampaging,
All die peoples flee.

Die odder haz a channel, too,
Vrom die lips to die brain.
It steggers theologians,
Causing all die schtoodents pain.

Die two of dem shud meet some day
und dis iss how shud be:
Die Moldau shud juz take Dalmau
Und vash him oud to zee!

The Candle's Flame

The candle is new,
Only recently lit.
Its sides are smooth,
Its rim, yet to split.

The flame, so young,
Won't dare to blink
For fear of what
The shadows might think.

I watch the fire.
The flame enhances.
I study the wall.
The shadow dances.

My heart is warmed.
I'll caress its light.
My hand draws near.
It warps with fright.

Little flame, don't fear.
My hand won't chill.
Let me touch your fire
And I will love you, still.

Journal entries:
Oct. 2, 1950

Great is the joy of giving!

Oct. 9, 1950

It has taken only a week to forget completely how great is the joy of giving.

Last week I had some candy bars and gave them away. It was difficult to decide to do so, but the return of joy was well worth the trouble. *Parva bona data datori melius gustant* – "Small goods, when given away, taste better to the giver."

I realized that God wanted some little things from me – self-denials and the like – and I tried to imagine the joy it would give God to have me give Him some, and how much I, too, would enjoy it.

Undated:

"Pray, pray very much. Make sacrifices for sinners. Remember that many souls are lost because there is nobody to pray and to make sacrifices for them."

Our Lady of Fatima.

From Miles Away

From miles away and years apart
God sent me you to warm my heart.
That finding you I'd learn to love
The shadow of my God above.

So, teach me to dance as you taught me to smile,
And I'll whirl you away an eternal while.
Come, be my date. Let's rendezvous.
On that far away shore, I'll wait for you.

Though you might linger and come very late,
My heart will lie waiting outside the gate.
I'll hug you but once, just wait and see,
And I'll kiss you but once, for eternity.

Till then I must love you, all sight unseen,
Content with a memory, as often I've been.
Come, follow me, monster. Come rendezvous,
My puppy, my pumpkin, my wonderful you.

Less than Three

Loretta paused and left a kiss
So downy soft she seemed to miss.

She hovered high upon her toes
And kissed with chin and lips and nose.

So little girls with artless grace
Will leave a kiss upon your face,

Then shyly turn and take to flight
When less than three in age and height.

Character

Ember to ash.
Ember to flame.
Credit the wind?
The winds were the same.

Home from College

When I came home from college,
I went to see my girl.
I had flunked the first semester
'Cause my mind was in a whirl.

She had sent back all my letters
And didn't read a one.
So I chose to go and see her,
To learn what I had done.

That evening was a failure
Right from the very start.
I offered her a choc'late kiss,
and then she broke my heart.

My ring was on her dresser
With half a dozen more.
My picture and her make-up
Were sharing one small drawer.

The telephone kept ringing
The whole time I was there.
She said it was a girlfriend,
Then squirmed some in her chair.

So, I told her I had things to do,
And couldn't wait to start.
I left with just my choc'late kisses
And an empty, broken heart.

Journal entry:
Undated

Serious as I am now, it occurs that I am certainly an oafish ass at times – loudmouthed, sharp, cruel, mean in my speech, speaking before I think twice. Why, if not to cover up, stamp down or exalt one thing or another? What have I to hide or get rid of, but imperfection and sinfulness?

God's Earthworm

The summer day was very hot
And, on the ground, lay just a dot:
God's earthworm.

The sun beamed strong. The soil was dry.
The tiny creature began to cry:
God's earthworm.

And looking up, to God he prayed,
He wept and begged the pain allay
for God's earthworm.

God heard the cry, love unrestrained
from on High and, so, it rained
On God's earthworm.

Now, in the garden of your life,
The rain's God's grace to help your strife.
The soil in the story is your convent or sem.
The place God gave to earn your diadem.

You're no earthworm!

Journal entry:
February 4, 1951

The will is very pliable, in a sense. Practice molds it. Practice doing the good (which is hard) and the discipline strengthens it. Practice doing the evil (which is easier) and the will is weakened, even when the evil is assented to under a false perception of good. But God's will is the ultimate good, and He gives His Graces only for the practice of serving His will.

To The Girl, Way Back

A man built a house
And then, one day,
Set down his tools
And walked away.

Along the trail,
Each time he would rest,
He professed to all,
"My house is the best."

He travelled far
And met a wench,
A lovely girl
Who shared his bench.

She studied his words
And motioned him back,
Then clapped her hands
With a *clack, clack, clack.*

"Your home's unfinished.
Your house isn't done.
Go back and see.
Oh, try me, for fun."

So he retraced his path
And wended his way
'Till he came to the house
He had bragged on, that day.

He inspected the structure
As he moseyed around,
Scanning each detail
From gable to ground.

And suddenly, there,
He saw the lack:
A single shingle,
Low in the back.

Then he made the repair
But he could not stay.
It was, still, not a home.
So, he ambled away.

He returned to Cathy,
The girl way back,
And offered the keys
To his humble shack.

FALL

After seminary, Duncan joined the Catholic Order of the Brothers of Our Lady of Mount Carmel, professing solemn vows of poverty, chastity and obedience. This commited him to a strictly structured future lifestyle. From then on, he would be associated with, and submissive to, a community of Carmelites – owning nothing, sharing everything.

However, his Spiritual ambitions had not yet been fulfilled. So, on May 28, 1955, Brother Duncan received the Sacrament of Holy Orders and was ordained a priest, forever.

At that time, his primary responsibilities evolved into another joy: teaching. Now, everything seemed to be coming together in the life for which he had hoped. Those hopes, however, would be short-lived.

To Jeannie, Caught Wincing

Why the look of sadness?
Your smile has taken flight.
Wince not when your playmate taunts
That you were born at night.

Though your skin is swarthy,
Your hair is black as jet,
Your smile, to me, is sun-bright.
Little one, do not fret.

My habit too is darksome
But it earns your love for me.
So, shall I don a brighter one,
Or discontented be?

No, my pretty darkling,
This dark shade I'll always wear,
May I that, with half the grace,
As you and your jet black hair.

Journal entry:
Undated

I long to have children of my own. That is only nat-
ural. So, it is good to remember, once in a while,
that choosing celibacy is a noble path. It is a grace-
filled gift from God, that we are able to freely deny
ourselves the pleasure of the marriage act.

The difficulty in choosing celibacy is not so much
the loss of licit pleasure or even the bond of a life-
long love. But to forego marriage as the source of
children, that seems to me to be the most hard.
There are other children, of course, but you can-
not hug them, knowing, "flesh of my flesh, my son
… my daughter."

Love of our children is ultimately love of ourselves.
Yes, it is selfish, but God-ordained and, therefore,
an honorable selfishness. But we – the eunuchs for
Christ – are enabled to free ourselves even from
this honorable selfishness. We are not automatical-
ly purged of all self-love. Rather we are set beside
ourselves, between ourselves and God. And to one
or the Other we go completely.

Once I consider how exalted the state celibacy is, I
am quite amazed that I chose it, even prompted by
the grace of God. But when I consider that young
girls – my very own sisters – have done the same, I
can only praise God for His Goodness; I can fath-
om the depths of such a mystery with only one
plumb-line – God's Love, which is His Mercy, His
Goodness, Himself.

Now, all shall be my children and I, their father.

My Choice

Some choose to endure
The bustling streets,
Where the cars roll by
In unending fleets,
Where the bird exists,
But seldom tweets.

Some choose to settle
In a cool, shady dale,
Where the night is garbed
In a blue-white veil,
Where the clouds steal by
On a distant gale.

Some choose to dwell
In highland atmosphere,
Where the air is chill
And the sky is clear,
Where the glaciers yield
To the mountaineer.

But I choose to live
On the soft, sloping shore,
Where the billows break
And the breakers roar,
Where the sandpipers flit
And the seagulls soar.

Journal entry:
Undated

The sincere religious makes sacrifices, realizing that mortification of self is necessary for Perfection. But all too often Perfection appears as a distant goal and not as a demanding, urgent, and present necessity. Our attempts at mortification tend to be sporadic and short-lived, occurring only when we have been forcibly reminded of our duty to strive manfully after Perfection.

Mary gives us a motive that will (after serious meditation) move us to make sacrifices. Yet, making sacrifices for sinners does not eliminate the motive of Perfection which is, more than a motive, an essential effect of persevering mortification performed for Christ's sake.

We realize that, due to the lamentable condition of Human Nature, sinners have always existed, they exist now ... and we are among their number! Therefore, we should never forget that our mortifications of self benefit us all.

Journal entry:
Undated

Mary's acceptance was enlightened and un-limited. For similar faith and trust God will soon be at work in the soul of such a one, unseen, but there, as surely as He was in the womb of His Mother once she said "Yes." Our sole concern has become to get God so as to give God.

The Christmas Pine

There was a little pine tree
All white and bent with snow.
It grew upon a hillside
Two thousand years ago.

And as the snow kept falling,
'Till not a spot was bare,
Thru the town that stood nearby,
There trudged a weary pair.

From inn to inn they wandered.
They sought a bed in vain.
"No room for you, try somewhere else,"
echoed down the lane.

The pair of weary travelers
Then spied upon a hill
A stable near a pine tree,
A shelter from the chill.

As they approached the stable,
The snow had ceased to fall,
The skies, first cloudy, now were clear,
And starlight beamed on all.

Inside the shelter, damp and dark
The pine tree could not go.
And, yet, he knew that Christ was there,
For an angel told him so.

The little pine was all alone
Beneath the stars outside.
He wondered if he'd be forgotten,
His branches drooped, he cried.

But Jesus loved the tree so well
He graced its highest limb
By putting there an angel
To protect the tree for Him.

And there he sits this very day,
Upon each Christmas tree,
Our Savior's guardian angel
That He gave to you and me.

Elevator Games

I've had enough,
You mechanical clown!
I want up,
But you go down.

I'll play your game,
Disagreeable pup.
I'll press down.
Now, you'll go up.

Kathy

God gave Kathy sparkling eyes,
Humor, poise and grace.
He blessed her with a lovely soul
To match her lovely face.

Health, God gave her, kindness, too,
Love — and not the least.
He let her have an Uncle Dunc
To be her own pet priest.

Does she ever stop to think
Though, He leaves her free,
God grooms her as His special love,
His darling bride-to-be?

Journal entry:
Undated

Dear God, help me be humble. Let my present pride be as part of general immaturity and be banished with effort and the passing of time. But my effort, O God, is nothing. It serves only to rattle the knocker on the Great Door, to let You know I am there, seeking entrance. You must give me the battering-ram. I want to come in, but I am feeble, weak, and inconstant. Had You not let down the drawbridge I would have surely fallen into the moat. I am so feeble and inconstant that I can scarce knock long enough to gain entrance for my importunity.

You seem to be waiting for me to say, "Lord, without You I can do nothing. Well I say it, Lord! But I can't seem to impress it on myself completely, even though I acknowledge my commitment, verbally. In all things I am proud, self-centered and arrogant. Few, if any, see the little boy in me who is seeking to grow in love. Most only know the self-centered, noisy kid who was repressed years ago for lack of friendship, but who is now wiser but more subtly self-centered than children.

Dear God, I accept all things from Your hands — persecution, sickness, insanity , all manner of trial, and death. Only help me to arrive at the fullness of love for You that my heart is capable of. Help me to help myself, and help me to help others. Finally, help me to stop the blurting of my big mouth.

The Message

From high above,
A sign of love,
To here below,
Falls drifting snow.

Swirling, now, up
And then around,
Making not
the slightest sound.

The brush of God
Paints all things white,
Rendering
A most beautiful sight.

On dormant trees clinging,
The message He's bringing:
"All, be of good cheer,
For Christmas is near!"

Journal entry:
March 1, 1951

To become a saint one must have a will that is disciplined to obedience, a will that is docile to every prompting of God's Grace. In following God's lead, our lives become holy and, as you live, so shall you die. Therefore, the prime necessity to became a saint is a disciplined will.

Is This the Lake?

A child was shown a lake one day
When it was mirror-flat.
This was the first real lake he'd seen,
So he studied it as he sat.

Nothing budged, up in the air
Or in the depths below
To make the mirrored images
Begin to ripple and go.

Each tree, each barn, the sky, the shore
Were mirrored in the lake.
So very real (but upside down)
Just like his favorite cake.

"Is this the lake, or this the lake?"
The little boy had wondered.
"Is this the lake, or this the lake?"
And, far away, it thundered.

Then came wind and, with it, waves,
Together, they pounded the shore.
The little boy looked all about
But the images were no more.

And so he cried the whole way home
He sobbed and wept all day.
He told his mother through his tears,
"Pretty lake just went away."

The Rose

I watched a rosebud, pale, unfold.
From bud to bloom it sped.
And, in between, the rose, it blushed,
Until its petals bled.

For as it passed from bud to bloom
It thought, "My beauty goes."
But One who watched,
He understood,
And whispered, "No, it grows."

The rosebud broader smiles each day,
Deep red, its color flows.
It blushes, still, its beauty mounts.
My God, I love this rose.

Journal entry:
February 22, 1953

It is easy enough for those who have felt death –
or imagined they felt it – to see the similarity be-
tween death and dying to self. When fearing death
we focus on words unsaid and plans undone. We
think of our loved ones and wish we could leave
them with words of consolation for those who will
be deeply grieved by our passing. But, at last, we
become reasonable, seeing all these anxieties as
useless. Then, we recognize that we are turning to
face God, rather than turning away from life.

In physical death there is a complete break, once
and for all. In death to self, however, we struggle
daily with our habits and tendencies, longing to
retain our "creature comforts." So, death to self
must be approached as a continual ideal because
our evil habits constitute a primary motivator in
life. If death to self were to be effected by a single
act of the will, how many more saints would there
be? But habits must be fought continually. This
struggle separates "the men from the boys." With
God, we can repudiate our evil habits, even though
it may take a lifetime to find that strength of will.

We are best served, however, when we recognize
that the time to turn toward God is now. We
should begin this walk toward Him, even if we
start our journey, limping from the burdens of our
sins.

WINTER

During the winter of his life, Father Duncan suffered through the Dark Night of the Soul that St. John of the Cross – a fellow Carmelite – had described, and many saints have faced. He experienced no loss of faith, but a profound, depressing impotence, much like Jesus Christ must have endured when He uttered the words: "My God, My God, why have You forsaken Me?"

Father's decline had been severely debilitating. However, he prayerfully managed to regain enough strength to allow for two hopeful pilgrimages to Lourdes, including one blessed with a side trip to meet Pope Paul VI at the Vatican.

Brother Mine

Why serve me not, brother mine?
You dislike me, or things Divine?

Can your hate be this intense?
God knows, I gave you no offense.

But had I that, you would still serve:
For quarrels make no Christian swerve.

You were God's candle. On you, His mark.
Now you are flickering, tempting the dark.

So, are you Adam, concealed in the trees,
Hiding offenses from Him who sees?

Flicker no more. Your light now grows dim.
I barely distinguish your candle's white rim.

Please cease your flicker, brother mine.
What can I do to help you shine?

Journal entry:
June 3, 1951, Retreat

We must find God in ourselves before we can find or see Him in others. When we fail to find God in ourselves, we end up praying to plaster and, therefore, not at all.

Journal entry:
Undated

Illness tries one's faith with endless questions of "Why?" Have I no value to others, to humanity, to the Church at large, to the pious souls who plead for prayers? Am I just a "good example" for people to witness?

But, eventually, when we are finally ready, God "commands the waters" and there comes the great peaceful calm. That is, since we cannot now know the answers to these questions in the normal course of events, we must live by faith.

So, illness can beget a deepened faith, a belief in the goodness of God, and a great trust, an enlightened and unlimited permission for God to work His will in the murky depths of our souls and throw on the lights, as He pleases, to let us glimpse the progress we have made.

When God is at work, we trust Him, even when, to our eyes, we seem to make no progress or to retrogress. Ultimately nothing is of any serious concern, except God's glory.

"I am Who am."

A chord has been struck, an *arpeggio* given. What will follow? A harmony, a melody, or discord? Even as illness of body attempts to grasp our spirit, shall we not allow God to snatch it back?

Journal entries:
May 30, 1963
[While sick with a persistent fever and after another run-in with an uncompromising Prior, he wrote:]
What an unbearable place this has been for the last six years with this – let's leave it at "Prior" – a real hell hole, a pious hotel, a penal colony.

Two days later:
The fever is more continual now, and it rather saps the strength out of you, and the will – if any remains – to do anything but rest. The ear's verging on ache. Removed a polyp from my tongue.

Then, on June 11, 1963:
I went to the hospital today, recurrence of Hodgkin's most probably being the trouble. Low grade fever, some sluggishness, a few local aches.

An Executioner Repents

The sun has set,
A silhouette
Is in the western sky.
A barren hill,
Three crosses still,
All meet my weary eye.

I near the gate.
It's getting late.
I cast one long last look.
I see His cross
And feel the loss
Of Him whose life I took.

I hear His voice.
He says, "Rejoice."
I see one thief relax.
I hear a cry,
Up in the sky
a peal of thunder cracks.

Lo! Jesus Christ
fulfilled His tryst,
Hangs dead upon the cross.
Dark death He braved,
Our souls He saved,
All else to Him was dross.

My eyes now burn
As I discern
His garments in my fist.
And kneeling down
Outside the town
I pray for what I'd missed:

"I ask Thee, Lord,
Replace my sword
With cross of solid oak.
Oh, would that I
Were now on high
With Thee whose heart I broke!

Lord, promise me
That You will free
My heart and soul from vice,
And join me to
Thyself Jesu,
On high in Paradise!"

How Gray Is My Night

Out and away,
Flickering gray,
My night is slow
To fade.

Droplets of dark
Catching their mark
From leaf to leaf,
Cascade.

Gabels of stone
Point to the groan
Of an airplane passing,
Unseen.

Here in the near
I can still hear
The far away thunder
Careen.

Mid-winter Memory

No more to swing from russet trees,
No longer riding autumn breeze,

Once garnishing a faded lawn,
Now, even deprived of the daily dawn,

Low they lie, and covered with snow,
Lively green leaves, but a season ago.

Journal entry:
Dec. 11th 1963

[After years of cancer treatments and deteriorating health, the psychological strain became apparent. Father Duncan experienced his "Dark Night of the Soul."]

Illness has made me selfish. Illness has isolated me. I have no plans of practicing the social graces every night as a remedy. I do think, "why bother – you're half dead and do not have the time to eradicate a habit of such long standing." I see myself as sharp-tongued, critical and therefore alienating. Why? Because it was the easiest adjustment for a shy, sensitive, quiet, but aggressive person to make to life in general but in particular to jungle life in the seminary, or should I say desert life?

No classmate of mine writes to me or I to him. I'm sick. So what? I'm well again. So what? I go it alone. I say this not by choice, but by recognition. I label a situation and I'm not broken up about it. It's all just part of knowing myself. Thank God that I know Thee. Without You it wouldn't mean a thing, but would be good cause for despair, insanity or suicide. Knowing You, I find this all a job to be done, not a curse. This is a challenge, not a threat; a temporary lack of sanctity, not an unalterable, intolerable reality.

It is a sad, sorry boast, but apart from the grace of God I made it alone. I did the damn-near impossible. I made it alone – without the favor of the Rector, without the crutch of a clique, with few enemies, but with no close friends, I made it. Alone. And to this day, I go it, alone.

Eulogy for a Priest

Three wars there are,
Every man must fight:
The holy war
'Gainst the devil's might,
The noble resistance
of the world's delight,
And the battle of the flesh.

The first two wars,
Rarely seen by men,
Are fought within
Soul's deepest den.
The third is more visible,
Now and then:
'Tis the battle of the flesh.

We never saw him
fight dark powers,
Nor resist the world,
In his private hours.
But his blessings were clear
As springtime showers,
Even when he battled with the flesh.

We saw him fast
In the banquet hall.
Played us, shot for shot,
In basketball.
A hundred other things,
We saw them all,
Until his battle with the flesh.

To you now be
The joy of victory
Most Reverend Master,
Father Malachy.
To those now be
The guilt of calumny,
Who forget your conquest over the flesh.

Journal entry:
Undated

We have something to offer that is worthy of Him: not passivity or a limited pliancy of soul, but full operation of our faculties of mind and body – in so far as this is possible – so that we are indeed Sons of God in communion with Him. Only then can we return to God the single gift worthy of God.

Journal entry:
Jan. 31, 1964, 11:15 P.M.

Early this morning I began reading Mgr. Deery's book about Lourdes. Very fine read. I've decided to go back to Lourdes, subject to the permission of Superiors and certain necessary indications, namely sufficient health and money. I've been feeling well all day in spite of some coughing and some awareness in the hip and low back.

Alone, Afloat

Alone, afloat
In an endless sea.
The gray sky's above,
Black water's beneath me.

In vain, I search for
Something to bless:
Gulls, fish or flotsam,
I couldn't care less.

But, alas, there is, here,
Nothing to love,
But the sea below
And the sky above.

Therefore, I must wait,
Oh, so patiently
For when there is more
Than water, sky and me.

Sister Novice

As I lie here, on my death-bed,
Fifty years a nun professed,
Twelve o'clock tolls from the steeple.
I close my eyes in search of rest,

To slumber's arms I hasten gladly.
Dream I've slipped and had a fall.
Wake up dressed in white, and kneeling,
Chanting loudly in my stall.

"Pater Noster," I had started,
Skipped 'secreto,' said the rest,
Felt a hundred eyes stare thru me,
Tried to say I'd done my best.

Look! It's mealtime. I'm on penance,
Holding up a broken plate.
Three white cups and three white saucers,
All had met the selfsame fate.

As I lie here, on my death-bed,
Fifty years a nun professed.
Asking God to hear my prayers, but
Not to think that I'm a pest:

"Jesus, I'll be coming soon
With my saucers, cups, and plate,
And I dare to ask admission
To Your heavenly Novitiate."

One bell tolls from the steeple.
One more Sister passed the test.
'Sister Novice' died that morning,
Fifty years a nun professed.

Duncan's letter, from one dying priest to another:
February 23, 1964

"... by acceptance, I become priest and victim, as
Christ was."

Upon the Death of a Friend's Mother

O swollen eyes of sorrow, cease,
Thy vain attempts to hide thy woe.
Such recalls a shattered peace
Foretelling sadness, all must know.

So, thus it is, man's heart is made:
To lisp aloud some likeness of love.
My tear-fed words do quickly fade.
Your Nan's short life was from above.

Would that my words give heart relief
To wander freely 'cross verdant moors,
Where joy and sorrow fuse belief,
But who can know a woe like yours?

My hidden tears won't fitly mourn
Your lovely mother's untimely death.
We both now wait with patience born
From God's creative, loving breath.

Journal entry:
Retreat, June 3 to June 4 1951

At the opening conference, Father Hardy spoke of the necessity of making a retreat and of praying for oneself regularly, especially during retreat. A retreat is to prepare oneself for death, for "as you live..."

So, it is necessary to know how to live in order to die well. But, equally important, one must learn why God made us: to know, love, and serve Him in this world, and to be happy with Him in the next.

Of course, the best way to know another human being is to live with him. Christ is a human being. Live with Him! Communion and Mass should be the high point of every day, and the rest of one's hours should be a time of preparation and thanksgiving for the awesome gift of Communion with God.

Untitled

What is life —
No more than strife —
When we know not
Why we live it?

Journal entry:
Undated

Yesterday when we said the Office of St. Monica I was greatly moved, thinking both of Mom and the coming Mother's Day. I was moved not with self-sympathy, but toward a disgust with all things, but dying and going to God.

I feel unqualified for anything in this life, least of all for suffering, but I wish I could be *consummatus in brevi, explevit tempora multa,** and be *raptus est.*** Suffering seems the shortest way. For the rest, it all seems an enduring marking-time with the will of God till our time comes. I am detached from all things, but novelty can sometimes so fill my mind with vain, empty thoughts and imaginings that I wonder what God and Mom and Pop must think when my feeble prayers ascend to heaven, a spectacle to God, angels and men.

This life is so damnably repetitious, yet so dreadfully interesting in its unfathomable intricacies, and so wonderful in its happiness, that it seems there must be another life, somewhere, with all the contradictions, mysteries and frustrations of this life removed, revealed and relaxed. And for that other life, somewhere, I yearn with the deepest affections of my heart. "Thy Kingdom Come!" for me, and my brother and sisters.

**A Latin excerpt from Wisdom 4:13-14 which reads, in its entirety: "Having become perfect in a short while, he reached the fullness of a long career, for his soul was pleasing to the Lord."*
** *Latin for "caught up."*

Domino Hospital

Dawn ain't yet.
Patients get
Washcloths cold,
Then are told
Priest is coming.
Hear the drumming?
Ice and steel,
And the squeal
Of squared wheels
While cart appeals
For some oil,
As its toil
Goes urewarded,
But recorded.
Up with shades.
Now sun, in spades.
Then the scurries.
Sister hurries.
Father's come.
My Body's numb.
I briefly pray,
My God, to stay
In this slum.
Then I succumb
From outside din
To peace within,
And back to sleep,
But much more deep.
It's always so
In Domino.

The Negative of a Nurse

Her voice had great volume for one and for all
For bedside and station, for out in the hall.

"Bed One has a fever," She coldly intoned,
"And all night I listened to Bed Two groan."

"Bed Three is abusive. Bed Four has C.A.,
Bed Five is just faking and ruined my day."

She passed on her pills and left for her break,
While shooting a glare at the Bed Five fake.

Showed no one a kindness, wiping beaded brow,
Hers never was, but the patients'? Well, now!

All night long she had parked in her station
Eating the candy she had conned from a patient.

Doctors, she treated, as if to serve her,
And soon they stopped trying to unnerve her.

Heartlessly lazy, selfish was she.
The opposite of what she had trained to be.

Hiding behind wilted peaks and tarnished pins,
Fig leaves to cover her nursing sins.

Some day you'll know it. And what could be worse,
Than to one day discover you're the "Neg" of a nurse?

**Journal entry:
January 2, 1964**

Dr. Reiser has two or three times now tried to tell me about a special book he's reading. I think he's trying to intimate to me that time is about up. I'm taking an antibiotic for the fever and lung congestion It could be just a local infection, but it may well be the beginning of the final onslaught of Hodgkin's. God's will be done. February 11 seems a long time off, but it would be a nice day to die (or a nice day to be cured.)

Merit

*Softly God now whispers proof,
A loving life earns a diadem.
Who was ever helped by me
That I was not blessed by them?*

Final Mass

Now I offer my final Mass,
Wherein I am Priest —
A victim —
Till I succumb
To the mystical chemistry
That makes me Christ-y.

Journal entry:
Nov. 5, 1963

I was admitted this afternoon. Tomorrow morning I get mustard [cancer treatment].

Reading more of The Living Flame, earlier this evening, I came to a few tentative conclusions. One: I believe that I have fulfilled any obligation to pray for a cure, and to continue doing so now would be less than perfect on my part. I have long wondered whether I should pray for a cure – with, I believe, the best of intentions. I have persisted until now because praying for a cure has focused my prayer life on the goal of fulfilling my vocation as a priest.

But a cure is not a *sine qua non* [a necessary requirement] of my faith. In fact, the way of cure is really longer, more dangerous and arduous than illness. Illness is safer for, generally speaking, all things are meted out to try the body and the spirit. That is, to say, that there are no, or few, decisions on my part, pertaining to illness.

But then, along came John – St. John of the Cross – with his Living Flame. From that, I derive my Tentative Conclusion Two: The pliancy of my soul, which has been effected in me until now by illness, must not be wasted in complacent passivity. I mean something greater is in store. My not too tentative conclusion is to let God get on with this pliancy of soul He has begun to produce, and do with me what He likes. By "let God" I mean I actively must dispose myself, with His help, to allow Him full freedom, not just over my body, but over my soul, even as He empowered men with full freedom over His Body.

Until now, it has been as though I let God hold the tail of a race horse: my will. I must not just share the reins and saddle. (This is spiritually impossible and rough on race horses.) I must not aim at giving Him a ride or making Him the jockey. I must give Him the horse outright, so He can strip it of saddle and bit, leaving it with the greatest freedom possible. This gives me great optimism. If by my reading and re-reading a few pages of St. John of the Cross, God can so quickly "turn on the lights," wow! A cure is unnecessary, speaking absolutely.

Keep the will honestly informed and pliant in God's hands and we reap His angel-sung promise: "Peace to men of good will." Not, it occurs to me, sweetness and delight, but the peace of internal harmony.

Journal entry:
June 11, 1964

On May 16th I "escaped" from St. Joseph's Hospital, after 10 weeks. Thank God my strength has returned. I can walk up a flight of stairs and keep going when I get there without too much panting. The coughing has virtually stopped. I have good color – a tan – on my arms and face. In short I'm ready to leave for Lourdes June 15th with Fr. Colman, my present Prior. The only hitch – tumors in the right lower jaw and neck, one big fellow the width of a half-dollar directly beneath the ear, a smaller one down lower. Also some in the left pectoral area, almost under the arm. I am very hoarse due no doubt to the tumors. I get periods of weakness from two to three hours after eating, sometimes sooner, when I must sit or lie down and rest or sleep. I thank God for this timely respite much like the nice ones I had in the warm Fall. Just the feel of the breeze on the patio, the rustle of bushes, the warmth of the sun. Brother Ass appreciates all these, and the beautiful aromas from the blossoming shrubs. And the total lack of any problems. Not a care in the world! And what an appetite! It's the cortisone, I'm sure. Food tastes good and more tastes better. Almost natural beatitude. If I get to heaven – and I trust I will – I'll be a charity case at this rate.

[In this journal, just one more entry was posted, a month later. It briefly described the new medications Father Duncan would be taking.]

One Last Poem

Tosser of word-salads,
Too lazy to find rhyme,
Wielder of mind images,
Ten of them to a line.

typographical trickster,
low-casing some of my work.
Now, I'm punctuating...
according to a quirk!!!

This prosaic poetry
Is all that I have proffered.
Some observers call it junk,
'Cause that is what I've offered.

My crude jottings have become
A final "masterpiece."
(Did I really start to believe
It was ready to release?)

So, take this one last poem
And file it with my stash
Or, better yet, in the bin
That has the label: "Trash."

And now that I have skewered it,
This long and skinny column.
May my final monument show
True words that are quite solemn.

Gather 'round and begin to read
Wisdom's grand epitaph.
In the words of one last poem:
"He winnowed the wheat. He sold the chaff."

ETERNAL SPRING

DECEMBER 16, 1964

Fr. Duncan's Prayer

O Mary Star of the Ocean,
To thee I pledge devotion,
And through thee, precious Mother Mild,
To thy sweet and loving Child.

While in this life, my way I wend,
Joseph, help my days to end
With thee and Mary by my side,
And Jesus near, my steps to guide
homeward, heavenward,
to gates thrown wide.

Father Duncan was the youngest of five Reilly siblings and the first to die. He carried with him these pictures of his brother and sisters. Clockwise, from top left: Malcolm, Jeanne, Marianne and Rosalie.

> "...nothing suffered for God's sake —
> no matter how small it be —
> goes without its reward."
>
> From *The Imitation of Christ*
> by Thomas a' Kempis

Rev. Duncan Reilly, O. Carm.
December 15, 1930
December 16, 1964
Saint Googie?

Background images courtesy of commons.wikimedia.org

Dedication pages: Snug Falls 2 by J.J. Harrison (jjharrison89@facebook.com)

Pages 8-9 and 86-87: Cloud sky over Brest by Luca Lorenzi

Pages 10-11: Switzerland Kanton hausen by Hansueli Krapf

Pages 12-13: Spring Fields at UCSC by Dylan Duverge' from Santa Cruz, USA

Pages 14-15: Spring Daffodils Barn Field by ForestWander

Pages 16-17: Sky Rift by Nicholas A. Tonelli

Pages 18-19: Sunspot by Axel Kristinsson

Pages 20-21: Late Summer by Nicholas A. Tonelli, Pennsylvania USA

Pages 22-23: Moon at its fullest by Thom Rains

Pages 24-25: Morning Sky by 4nachthorn

Pages 26-27: PuriSky by lovedimpy

Pages 28-29: Chender Kirschenbaum by Benjamin Gimmel

Pages 30-31: Big Summer Sky by Meena Kadri

Pages 32-33: Pumpkins field by Yvan Leduc

Pages 34-35: British Night Sky by Tom Bayly, England

Pages 36-37: Islands of the Cyclops at Dawn by gnuckx

Pages 38-39: Acapulco sunset summer by Arturo Mann

Pages 40-41: Afternoon sky by lostinfog

Pages 42-43: Beach near Carloway in summer 2012 by Chmee2

Pages 44-45: Morning Mist over the Lake by Harald Hoyer from Schwerin, Germany

Pages 46-47: Near New Belvidere (New Jersey) by Nicholas from Pennsylvania, USA

Pages 48-49: Paysage by moi

Pages 50-51: Morning Clouds by "chefranden"/Randen Pederson

Pages 52-53: Cloudy fall day on lake by Hagerty Ryan, U.S. Fish and Wildlife Service

Pages 54-55: Autumn trees cloudy sky - Virginia by ForestWander

Pages 56-57: Even fir trees are golden by Andrew Kudrin from Novosibirsk, Russia

Pages 58-59: Autumn mountain sky, sunrise colors - West Virginia by ForestWander

Pages 60-61: Red Rose by Aryan Paswan

Pages 62-63: Winter sky by Duncan Harris

Pages 64-65: Interstate 80 NW Utah by DR04

Pages 66-67: La croix de Loriaz by Geo75

Pages 68-69: Night sky stars trees by Michael J. Bennett

Pages 70-71: Winter landscape in Oberbayern (Bavaria) by sebastian. sauer

Pages 72-73: Seascape after sunset by Rodrigo Nuno Bragança da Cunha

Pages 74-75: Winteredammerung by attatrol47

Pages 76-77: Chasing the sun by Andrew Kudrin from Novosibirsk, Russia

Pages 78-79: Colours in the Morning by Luis Argerich

Pages 80-81: San Francisco Peaks during winter by Coconino National Forest

Pages 82-83: Tree shadow, Sanger by temporalata

Pages 84-85: Lobo seashore by Jojo Nicdao

All family pictures from collection of Jeanne Reilly.

CPSIA information can be obtained at www.ICGtesting.com
Printed in the USA
LVOW01*0203260713

344728LV00001B/1/P